The Project of Being Alive

Acknowledgements: Some of these poems have appeared in *Labyrinth, Mike Maggio's Poetry Month blog, Tele-woman, Puff Puff, Rat's Ass Review, Bridges Math-Poetry Anthology 2018.*

Poems

Marion Deutsche Cohen

Copyright©Marion Deutsche Cohen, 2018
Art Cover Copyright© *Subcutaneous. Dermis.*
(Oil on Canvas 30 cm x 50 cm) Devin Asher Cohen, 2018
Printed in the United States of America
All Rights Reserved
Published by Agreement with Summerfield Publishing,
d.b.a. New Plains Press,
216 South 8th Street, Opelika, AL, 36801
newplainspress.com

CATALOGING IN PUBLICATION DATA
American Poetry, Women's Poetry, Math Poetry, Poetry
Library of Congress Control Number
2018957980
ISBN 13: 978-0-9986857-5-5
Marion Deutsche Cohen 1943 -
Other books by Marion Deutsche Cohen:

Tuesday Nights, ed. with Wemara Dare, The Weirdest Is the Sphere, An Ambitious Sort of Grief, The Shadow of an Angel, The Temper Tantrum Book, A Garden Flower, Mother Poet, ed., She Was Born She Died, The Sitting-Down Hug, Counting to Zero, The Limits of Miracles, ed., The Level of Doorknobs, Extreme Points, These Covers to Crawl Under, Dirty Details: The Days and Nights of a Well Spouse, Epsilon Country, Crossing the Equal Sign, Surviving the Alphabet, Chronic Progressive, Parables for a Rainy Day, Still the End: Memoir of a Nursing Home Wife, Sizes Only Slightly Distinct, Lights I Have Loved, Closer to Dying, Truth and Beauty, and New Heights in Non-Structure.

THE PROJECT OF BEING ALIVE

Table of Contents

PART I: CURIOUS LIGHTS AND MATH

Curious Lights of Various Dimensions

Sometimes a point of light happened to coincide
with one of the upper corners of my room.
Other times a line of light coincided
with the intersection of wall and ceiling.
But rectangles of moonlight coincided with nothing and,
throughout the night, touched everything.

Three-dimensional lights didn't happen.

Except that one time.
It was the first curious light ever,
and it coincided with the entire room.

Earliest Memory, Under 2

Suddenly I thought "I'm there."
I was being put down for a nap.
And the sun refused to go away.
My room could not get dark.
God said, Let there be light
but not Let there be dark.

God meant
Let light exist.
And I meant, I exist.

Not quite existential horror.
But not quite existential joy.
Just-plain existential in the raw.

I didn't and don't wonder why I exist.
That isn't my main problem.
It's kind of the solution
the secret of the universe
the answer to any zen koan.

I wasn't even talking yet.
But I must have been thinking.
Maybe I had just begun to think.
I certainly didn't say, "I'm there."
All I said was, "Off, off."

Maybe God said Off off.
And maybe it was too late.
The light had become too big.
Big enough to get into everybody's room.
Big enough to get into everybody's nap.

Twelfth Birthday Party

It was a huge success. At least the other kids thought so. Someone had brought records, not Bach and Beethoven like my parents. Someone else was running the phonograph and everyone was dancing the jitterbug. I wasn't even a teenager yet and the birthday party I'd been so excited about had turned into something non-birthday. I'd known for at least a year that I wouldn't always be a child but I'd thought I'd have at least a couple more birthday parties.

Thirteen

My mother said How do you think it makes me feel to see my teen-aged daughter making clothes for clothespin dolls?

I was worried too. When was I going to stop being so interested in doll clothes? Or rather, when was I going to stop worrying about being so interested in doll clothes?

Answer to both questions: when I discovered thrift-shopping, for my clothes. At least once a week.

When am I going to stop loving thrifting so much?

Answer: never. How would my mother feel seeing her seventy-two year old daughter altering yet more thrift store clothes?

That Kitten

Mittens I came whenever we called her.
Mittens II called whenever we came to her.
Scattie looked like Hitler.
And Lilac was tiny and drying.
But I don't remember with which kitten,
I, thirteen, painful, hilarious, and self-dubbed
Junior Philosopher
alone in the house that 7:30 PM
sat in the big diagonal chair
and made up sad songs
both truly sad and affectively sad
while the air began to show more
and the furniture began to show less.

I don't remember to which kitten
I poured as she purred
yes, to which kitten I sang

of time
of space
of love
of not having loved at all
and, probably, existence
and the sum of the angles in polygons with crossing sides.

I was a young one
but I sang like an old one.
It was a long evening
as long as my future.
And whichever kitten arched,
yawned,
curled,
and slept

yes, listened the way I'd always
wanted to be listened to.

Philosophy 101

I'd thought philosophers were Tortured Souls, I'd thought they cried when they thought their philosophy, and I'd thought they thought their philosophy all alone. I hadn't known philosophy was something to take true/false tests in or write term papers on or discuss while the teacher brandished cigarettes. And I hadn't known other philosophers had thought the same things I'd thought, I'd thought at least I was alone.

Statement

A good teacher is supposed to teach students, not
 subjects.
But I teach math.
Whoever the students, math is the subject.
If there were no students I'd probably still teach my
 subject.
I'd teach and I'd learn all by myself.

First Adult Curious Light

It wasn't a point or a line.
And it wasn't a matter of coinciding.
It had simply crash-landed strictly inside the space above
 the bedroom closet.
Every 29 seconds it disappeared, for precisely 39 seconds.
Thirty years I had slept in that bedroom and not noticed
 the light had been there night after night.

I'd thought it was from a temporary car.
I was 72 when I deduced that it wasn't.
How can a light so persistent, so precisely
 intermittent come from such a car?
No, this light was something new.

I was 72 and curious.
I had to go to the window.
I had to see under what conditions it disappeared from
 the wall and appeared on my hand.
Where did my hand have to be, in front of what?
Never had I been so interested in experimental math.

I knew I would not have to stare throughout the night.
I would not have to keep opening my eyes.
I would not have to buy thicker curtains.
At age 72, I needed only satisfy my curiosity.
Once and only once, not again and again.

Second Adult Curious Light

Another night, another light.
One and only one.

Grammar-Conscious

I might not have ever managed to get even
a mention in the New York Times
but I've got something over some of their writers.
They write 'one wonders if.'
They write 'different than.'
They mix clauses with complete sentences.
Yes, perpendicular structure.

Grammar is very mathematical
which is why I'm good at it.
It's not only that sentences can get diagrammed.
It's the placing of commas, parentheses
and quotes, double and single
and then, deeply inside, double again.

A Theory of Curious Lights

> "Little lamb, who made thee?"
> -- William Blake

Little Light, who made thee?
"I am the un-made, the non-existent, the never-thought-
 of."
That's what curious lights are for.
They're the only way.

Four Questions about Curious Lights

Have they lost their mojo?
Am I too old for them?
Are there only a finite number of them?
Did writing about them make them go away?

Cats Watching Mathematicians Work

Mirage knows which points and lines I should draw, and he knows which ones I should not draw.

He sees emerging from my pen a neatly dotted line that seems to me auxiliary, but about which he's thinking,

"No! no! That one won't help. That one will hinder."
He could gently nudge my hand or nip,
ever so minutely.

But he prefers to keep mum.
Does he know I'll learn from my mistake?
Or does he simply like my mistake?

Is he thinking, it won't help but it's pretty?

The First Math Thing I Didn't Understand

The algebra text didn't have symbols that weren't numbers or letters and even in Math Club they didn't tell us about the Goldbach Conjecture. All the math for the layperson books in Barnes and Noble that I'd plop myself down under and with didn't have any math for the non-layperson. So it wasn't a matter of ego that I thought I could do any math. It was a matter of experience.

I had no qualms when that newsletter for high-school math enthusiasts gave an address for subscribing to Scripta Mathematica, and I wasn't disappointed when, weeks later, the light green cover of Scripta Mathematica was infested with symbols that weren't numbers or letters and inside were long otherworldly formulas definitely not meant for high-school math enthusiasts. It still wasn't a matter of ego. Just, now I knew there was math I couldn't teach myself, math that couldn't be mine yet, math beyond the corollaries to the vocabulary I had learned.

Now I knew.

Someone Else's Curious Light

When Elizabeth was little she used to stare at a recurrent night-flickering that she called her angel.

I know that angel. It was near the top of the wall to the right of her bed. It was a light with a shape, just asymmetric enough, something like a bending Christmas tree.

I don't think Elizabeth loved her angel. I didn't love my childhood curious lights, or not during my childhood. It takes maturity to love a curious light. It takes maturity to not have to stare at a curious light
       to just relax and exist with it side by side.

My Brand of Poethood

I feel nostalgic about everything: childhood, adulthood, past, present, future. Space, too, nostalgic about particular corners, particular thrift stores. O yes, I know nostalgia well, first knew it age 6 when we moved out of what I called the country, no more green house with the red roof, no more infinite fields of Queen Anne's lace, no more no school. Knew it again, age 11, when I started junior high, whole different building, no more long lunches at home, no more friends who also liked to sit down and draw.

But that was bad nostalgia. What I feel as a poet is good nostalgia. Good nostalgia is like curious lights, Kroenecker's Extension Theorem, the last movement of Beethoven's last violin and piano sonata

bricks and Venetian blinds
preferred directions besides gravity
cellars beneath cellars
high-up cellar windows and slanted cellar doors.

Math Doesn't Come to Me This Summer

I thought I'd found a formula for a sharp associative and compatible with any star that satisfied those four properties with $m = 1$ and $n - 1$ prime. I'd even written down and checked the proof, almost finished typing it checking again as I typed. Everything jibed until Case IV Sub-case B and that couldn't be fixed. Now I've proved that for certain star there cannot be any commutative sharp associative and compatible with star. But that's a non-existence theorem, with too much hypothesis. Math just isn't coming to me this summer. Most summers at least one theorem — but so far this summer only that little lemma.

Last night, though. The full moon came to me. Suddenly, in the right window, there it just was. I stopped staring at the moon a long time ago, but last night I changed my mind. I wanted to see how fast it travelled, how long it would take to disappear behind the right wall. I lay with my head stark still, held in place by two pillows, and yes, just as I'd suspected, it took less than five minutes.

If I can't have math, I'll settle for the moon.

Vow

Usually I write more than one book about anything that
 happens to me.
And math happened to me.

Math courted me.
Math seduced me.
Math impregnated me.

Whither math goeth, I goeth
lawfully wedded
in sickness or in health
till death do us part.

The End of an Era

This is another insomnia night and I'm spotting another
 curious light.

But I'm not investigating.
It's curious, all right, but I'm not curious.
I don't have to know what it is.

From now on laziness takes precedence over curiosity.
And from now on I don't need curious lights to put me
 back to sleep.

I knew my childhood would end but I didn't know this
 would end.

I didn't know it would end this soon.

The Quilt

At my grandparents' house I slept under a thick quilt with a thin white cotton cover and in the center of that cover had been cut a big round hole so the heavy quilt could be taken out and just the cover washed. I'd crawl through that hole, deep inside, deep into the corners.

I don't remember whether it felt like my mother's womb or like Alice down the rabbit hole. Or whether there was a curious light in there. Don't remember much about then, all I know is now, now, when I think about it, it seems that was the most existential thing in my life.

And it wasn't. There have been math, pregnancy, birth, the babies themselves, other childhood memories, and dreams, and poems, and, yes, curious lights. Plus that evening my paralyzed paranoid suffering first husband finally died, it was some kind of eclipse.

And indoor windows. I mean both sides indoors, I have two of them right here in my house, I can have them any time I want just like I can write any time I want, just like I can think any time I want.

Just like, a long time ago, at my grandparents' house at night, I could crawl inside that quilt any time I wanted. Maybe that was the first thing I could do any time I wanted, the first thing I decided to do, again and again.

At Night the Window Becomes a Mirror

If you're inside there's no outside.
If you're outside there's no inside.
And you're happy to be stuck, happy to be living,
happy and secure in this half world.

Not the End of the Era

I have exhausted the curious lights in the bedroom.
But tonight I have wandered into the hallway.
And there, on the next door, shimmers something
 Y-shaped
something like a Jacob's Ladder.

I have to place my hand on it.
Then I have to move my hand back.
I have to follow this light
to keep it on my hand.
I follow it through the long hallway.
I am out on some limb.
Now I'm in the other room.
I'm getting scared.
This light is leading me somewhere new
not out the window
perhaps into some mirror.
I try to keep the light on my hand.
If I raise or lower it, the light disappears and I can't get
 it back.

Maybe the light is made of fire.
Maybe the light is a giant bug.
Maybe the light is poisonous.

And so I give up on this curious light.
I go back to bed, thinking perhaps tomorrow.
Perhaps tomorrow I'll acquire more expertise in
and some immunity to
poisonous curious lights.

Sports Unillustrated

(1)
In third grade gym I didn't get baseball, I thought you need-
ed only finish running from base to base before the outfield
people, I didn't know about being tagged, suddenly struck
out. And Donna Gardner in the outfield knew I didn't know
so she made a big deal of waiting between third base and
home for me to be running by her and then very leisurely
and theatrically she touched me with the ball. I don't re-
member the comedy, I just remember the drama, the rather
slow drama, at my bewildered expense.

(2)
Around the neighborhood I got baseball and kickball and
the various games we made up, and I was good maybe best
at all of them and if I didn't want to play I'd go inside and
practice the piano or sew or take a nap. Around the neigh-
borhood I never did anything I didn't want to do.

(3)
In school gym we didn't only play games, we were taught
marching, she made us march, it felt like the army, I didn't
know much about armies except I didn't want to be in one,
my father had to be when I was a baby, World War II, I was
only ten months old but I remember, I remember noticing
him gone.

(4)
I was great in badminton and ping pong but not tennis or
bowling, I've always had strong arms but never wanted to
pick up a tennis racket or bowling ball. Way too heavy, cer-
tainly too heavy to wield. When it came to tennis and bowl-
ing I was weak and lazy in my hands, when it came to bad-
minton and ping pong I was light in both hands and feet.

(5)
In seventh grade I'd never heard of soccer and when the teacher explained it, several times, I kept not getting it because I kept being bored and not listening. When we actually started playing I had no idea what to do. Becky says she never got soccer either, she still doesn't get it but my grandson Jack is absolutely perfect at it, he gets every possible goal. For my grandson Jack, what's the big deal?

(6)
In college I got fencing, I mean really got, I beat the teacher. But one thing I didn't get: what was the big deal? All you do is lunge, what was so hard about that? But I didn't get A in fencing, I got C because he gave a written Final and I guess I got C in it and I guess that's all he counted, I guess in fencing the correct answers lay in the word rather than the deed.

(7)
When Devin was four, I forty-six, we were walking along this street in West Philly when I spotted a bunch of young people playing volleyball, Ooo, that looks like fun, I said to Devin. I hadn't played volleyball in decades and then hardly at all, Hey, I called out, Can I join you? And I was so good at serving, I scored every time, like what was the big deal? Everyone wanted me on their team, I was the expert server, when the opposite team served I couldn't do a damn thing but serving was my specialty, serving was my abstract algebra, serving and only serving was the part of volleyball I got.

(8)
My daughter says that had to be a dream but Becky says Yep, serving, she also couldn't do anything else in volleyball but serve. Serving was our thing, something about serving, serving in the army hell no but serving in volley ball heavens yes.

(9)
And people who say they just-can't do math, there's usually some math they can do, some math is their serving. If we find that something they might be able to do more math, maybe all math. My students, one or two or more every semester, "I just-can't do math" so I make up math they've never seen before so they've never just-not been able to do it so they do, at least one math they can do, it's light math like badminton or heavy math like tennis, they serve it right back at me, service with a smile, they're at my service, they get this sport, they don't get tagged, don't get drafted, they're light in hands, feet, and head.

The Latest Curious Light: Trying Again

I did not succeed.
First I tried closing the door to the other room.
Then I tried tracing it again on my hand.
I wandered farther and farther.
And the light suddenly disappeared.
It wasn't on my hand and it wasn't on any door.
Had it gotten smaller?
Had it been absorbed in the cracks between my fingers?
This isn't a big deal.
I won't lose any more sleep over it.
It's only another hopefully delicious
last curious light.

A Curious Dark

At that Florida AirBnB our room had a ceiling fan. I never liked ceiling fans and that one got worse at night when, due to some unknown light, it doubled up with its shadow, ten big dark wings close above us. It wasn't enough for me to close my eyes, I needed to delve under the covers in case my eyes accidentally opened. There's that scene in The Babadook, "you can't get away from the Babadook," she dreams she wakes up to it intersecting with the overhead light directly above her.

Eventually I investigated. It was Jon's computer, that small circular light left on, one of those lights that enlarge shadows. So finally on the last night of our stay I covered up that light and got to sleep through, no more Babadook, I could get away from the Babadook. I could and I did.

The Attack of the Latest Curious Light

This latest curious light, the Y-shaped one I gave up on
I have realized I am afraid of it.
It's too sudden, too bright, maybe sharp like a knife.
It doesn't go bump in the night but it goes something.
When I leave the bedroom I know I will see it.
And it cannot be prepared for.

Every evening I close the door to that other room, the
 room it comes from or through.
I tell Jon I am doing this and why.
I tell him to be sure to leave that door closed and he
 smiles.
He knows me and my curious lights.

But I'm not saying I don't love that light.
I have, yes, stopped trying to trace it
stopped trying to follow it.
But I still kind of love it.
Because it's like my associative arithmetics.
It's something only I know about.
Or I know more about it than anyone else.

Part II: Our Lives Before Our Eyes

Before the Dentist
age 8

The dentist said I had great teeth so how come he had to keep checking up on them? And how come he kept drilling? And how come my sister didn't have to go? Was it because she was younger, or were her teeth greater than mine?

Okay, if I had great teeth, I might as well play with them, and that meant poke, from the inside out, especially the top front right. Maybe before the dentist I hadn't realized I even had teeth, so now I was discovering a goldmine.

And I mined, all right, I sure did mine and this is a just-so story about that slightly-buck tooth. I mined and mined until it became totally mine.

Quick Answer

When I was pre-seventh grade
and my parents always told me where to go next
and my teachers' praise was the highest to aspire to
and my Aunt Faygie was like a Grandma
(Grandma was also like a Grandma)
and nothing was a matter of popular
when I wasn't coming of age, not even a little bit–
what season was it?

Quick answer: it was spring.
Oh, I well remember the extremes
the white season, building an almost-finished snow fort
 in the backyard
ice skates that never quite fit
and not really wanting to go outside, anyway
but warming feet in my mother's oven

and the yellow season, going swimming
 as exciting as a birthday
buzzing fireflies and tiger lily fireworks and no school
Frances knocking on the side door at 9:00 PM,
 ready to go out and play
and my mother with her heart condition
 and no air-conditioning

and the brown season, leaves in gutters piled higher
 than they are now
falling into those leaves, never hitting the concrete
crunching those dead leaves with my hands and feet
and my sister's Back to School birthday parties.

But mostly it was the green season
my father's lawn mower, my mother's zinnia garden
kickball in the front yard, badminton in the back
the Sheridan Avenue gang sitting on the porch,
 sometimes with kittens
bird noises at dawn like tears of happiness.

Yes, throughout my childhood the season was spring.
Spring was the average.
Spring was the default.
Everything else being equal, it was spring.

A Hole in My Feng Shui

Yesterday I feng shui'd up the kitchen table, so what if I haven't read the entire *NY Times* or even the two back pages of *The Chronicle* and definitely so what if we haven't eaten all that iffy fruit or if I'm consolidating nuts with crackers? And I feng shui'd my bed, so what if I haven't finished all five of the poetry books teetering off the edge, and so what if I still haven't solved that math problem, if that partial-proof of many pages which went nowhere was just about to go somewhere?

So now things are relatively feng shui. But uh-oh, what about this eight-and-a-half by eleven here in my hands, little twiddly zigzags between the lines, words riddled with carots, margin all used up?

No, there's no local feng shui, not today and probably not tomorrow, no feng shui in this tiny corner, this two-dimensional hot potato stuck to my willing fingers, to my very willing self.

Turning 70

There is no theory of death that pacifies me. Dying probably feels like drowning or being upside-down too long. Don't put the sheet over me until you're sure I'm dead.

And now my psyche has registered 70. Now I dream "Hey, I'm 70 and pregnant!" Not 65 any more. 70 in the subconscious—it didn't take long.

And teaching dreams. I'm back to Advanced Engineering Mathematics, only there's more engineering than mathematics.

And more and more, lately, of non-recurring dreams. How does this dream differ from all other dreams? It's longer and more realistic. Yes, too much like not-sleeping. Too much like daytime, not enough like night.

Scene from That French Movie

In that Death Row nobody knew when.
But it was always the middle of the night.
At that particular 2:00 AM it was Pierre's turn.
It took awhile for them to wake him
and when they did he screamed
"NO! NOT TONIGHT! Please, not tonight. This is the first
 night I've been able to sleep."
Is death different from sleep? No one knows.
Is going to death different from going to sleep? Yes.
Definitely yes.

Moment of Truth

While I'm waiting to hear some verdict about something
 that is no longer in my hands
I can nonetheless cross my fingers.
It feels safe to those two fingers.
As though one were holding the other, or both holding
 onto each other.
I can even take one hand with its pair of crossed fingers
and cup it over the other hand
   with its pair of crossed fingers.
It's like people walking together in cold weather.
They can clasp, press, keep a kind of half
covered and warm.

That Whole Bad Year: 2001

So long a year had it been that I was surprised, each
 morning, when the sun rose.
And surprised each hour that it progressed across the
 sky.

Each rain that fell in the correct direction.
Each temperature on the thermometer
maybe irrational but never imaginary.
The sky only one sky or at least the farther sky didn't
 show.
Each object rigid, not changing shape or not fast enough
 to notice.
9:00 AM hitting right on the mark, not having been
 skipped.
And my appointment book still on the shelf, containing
 what I wrote.

Surprised that, although a poem could be rejected that I
 never submitted, a man couldn't break up with me
 whom I never dated.
And I couldn't wake up from a dream I never had.

The Silly Dream

At the tail-end of my deathbed I'll probably think,
 what a silly dream.
How could I ever have thought there was such a thing as
 being alive?
And not being alone?
And having a body? What on earth is a body? And that
 body loving other bodies?
Other bodies coming out of that body–how ridiculous is
 that? And friends for lunch?
What's friends? What's lunch?
How could I have believed such nonsense for so long?
Still, it was an interesting dream
a nice dream.
It made sense at the time.

Hard to Believe

It's hard to believe I'll never be young again and when I was young it was hard to believe I'd ever not be young. But even harder to believe: youth and non-youth come in two big clumps, can't they alternate? A few days of one with a few days of the other?

Things are so top-heavy. Against the laws of probability, against the laws of possibility. Like first all the even numbers, then all the odds. Something is out of order.

Every odd needs its even

within touch's reach

to rest and refresh it

get it ready

for the next odd.

The Long Haul

We're all pretty conscientious.
We finish what we started.
A long time ago we embarked on the project of being
 alive.
And we didn't abandon that project.
We keep eating.
We're never too lazy to eat.
We keep talking.
We usually know what to say.

Some of us are more conscientious than others.
Some, in the morning, widen our eyes sooner.
Others keep them narrow for awhile.
But we're all survivors
of the night and the morning.
We're all survivors
of the first part of our lives.

We knew ourselves when
and after all these years
we know ourselves now.

The Hardest Thing I've Ever Done

I was reading *The Secret Garden* to Elle, Arin, and Jill. I read it to them every time Jill slept over and as I was reading I was very happy, I held on to my uterus which contained Kerin. And I remember reading "the magic," over and over, "the magic, the magic," that had changed a little girl from surly and selfish to bright-eyed and caring, a little boy from wheelchair to frolicking, his father from aloof to joyful. "The magic," I read, "the magic." Maybe the author didn't write "the magic" as much as I remember, still "the magic" was something the four of us swayed to.

But as I was reading the last chapter I wasn't happy any more. Kerin wasn't in my uterus and she wasn't in our house either. And one of the hardest things I've ever done—and I thought that at the time—was say "the magic." Now it was bad magic, it had dried the placenta, made it betray Kerin and me, made it stop working before Kerin got out, big bad magic that there was obstetrics I hadn't known about. But that's not the tone of voice I read "the magic" in. I read "the magic, the magic" in the same voice as before. "Be brave," I thought. "You can be brave" and it was magic, good or bad, that I could.

Surviving Surviving

When survivors are finished surviving, when they're settled into deep survival, they have to find new things, things that don't need to be survived. So they find these things.

They're not always all that sure about these things but they find them anyway. Like the ending of one version of *Beauty and the Beast*, they have to get used to ordinary beauty. They have to get used to ordinary truth.

Even Closer to Dying

Lucky-7-oh, I say but I don't like the sound of it. It helps that this has been an unbelievably healthy winter. It helps that just two months ago a very young person said I look 30. And my doctor says he doesn't think we need to repeat the routine blood tests. Also, I'm my high-school height and not far from my high-school weight. And my hair is thinning but not greying, at least in certain mirrors. I don't like the sound of 70, but so far the sight, smell, taste, and touch are just fine.

Closest to Dying

When we're closest to dying, so close that our lives are
 passing before our eyes
we're seeing some wonderful things.
But we don't really want that kind of living.
We don't want to live so fast.
We don't want to live so alone.
And we don't want to live
with only our eyes.

The Long Haul, 2

We're still finishing what we started.
We have a ways to go.
And we're getting tired.

We don't want to stop.
We don't need a vacation.
But somebody, please, get us a grant.

Or some kind of scholarship.
At least pay us minimum wage.
We can't keep working on this project for free.

PART III: Bargaining with the Human Condition

Reading in a Dream

Someone told me that you can't read in a
dream because the part of your brain that reads
isn't in the part of your brain that dreams.

My brain is special.
It can read in a dream.
Well, this dream. Well, these words.

Well, it can dream it's reading in a dream.
Well, at this angle
this distance.

And there's music.
One drawn-out augmented fourth
the kind they have in horror movies.

Still. Look! I'm reading in a dream.
My special brain
is reading in a dream.

Counting in a Dream

My special brain can count to sleep
and once it counted to fall awake
but it can't count in the middle.
It can't remember to inductively follow.
It can't know what comes after 19.

In sleep's middle appear numbers but not counting
 numbers.
Each of these numbers stands in its space, before and
 after nothing.
My special brain cannot make sense of these word-
 numbers.
And cannot stop them.
Cannot rescue them from being alone.

The Fury of Housework

I slap at the bugs.
Wildly I dream.
Back and forth, like an old woman with a broom.
Or smack on down, like a rugged-individual
 with a board of wood.
My instructions are to destroy
whatever is small and dark.
This is a forest, I'm a hunter.
This is a field, I'm a soldier.
This is a back, I'm the scratcher.
This is Italy, I'm Mamma Mia.

I'm the bat, I'm the ball.
I'm both the *Old Man and the Sea.*

Bugs move.
Bugs carry germs.
Bugs are like dust.
Bugs look like crumbs.
Should I keep on doing this? If I do, I'm cruel.
If I don't, well,
maybe that's why people aren't allowed to live forever.
Because somebody up there doesn't want
to be accused of cluttering.

Dream of Telekinesis

It's not all it's cracked up to be.
The balls, for instance. I can't get them to roll in just any
 direction.
Only directly forward and directly back.
And the blanket.
Sure, it does tricks for me.
Ties itself in a knot, a bow, rolls itself up, makes figure 8s.
But it seems, often, discontent.
I do preface each request with "if you'd like," but it only
bows and assures me my wish is its command.

And the purse.
I put it to bed, but it has too many zippers
too many compartments. It's beginning, I fear
to resemble a machine. And now it flutters
now it jerks. In other words, lately
more and more, they also move when I don't ask them to
even when I ask them not to. Either way
I'd rather they simply stay put.
There should be something non-living, something non-me.
A child stirs
in her sleep, or not.
But objects are supposed to be good.
At least at night. At least at home.

I don't like this. Everything is an animal.
I coddle it, pet it
it rubs me, licks me
and I am beginning to tremble.

The Woman Mathematician

Her child has awakened, or half-wakened, in the late evening. He is sitting up and fumbling, picking at the blanket, running first the edges, then the middle, through his fingers. He is trying, she can see, to figure something out. And she knows what it is, to figure something out.

"Whatsamatter, Cutie?" she whispers, and he answers right away. "Freaky somehow got inside the blanket."

She smirks and laughs, but huddles. "Didn't you put Freaky into his cage before you went to bed?"

"Yeah I did," he murmurs, or half-murmurs, "but somehow he got inside the blanket anyway."

"Do you remember putting him in his cage?"

"I don't know what happened."

"He can't possibly get in the blanket, the blanket's all sewn up." Nonetheless she, too, begins to fumble. Finally she gently nudges her child. "Go upstairs and check and see if Freaky's in his cage."

Her child soon returns. "Yeah," he tells her. Then he settles and she stays.

"It's okay, Sweetheart. You're just tired, you're just dreaming." She tenderly shrugs, kisses half his face.

She checks the blanket again. Freaky couldn't be in two places at once. Or there couldn't be two Freaky's. Roots have multiplicities, singularities have multiplicities, but hamsters don't have multiplicities. Also, you can identify the two opposite corners of a square but you can't identify the underside of a blanket with the inside of a hamster cage.

"Don't worry, Bitties," she continues, whispering and stroking. "It's okay, Funny. Go to sleep now. It's okay, Sweetheart. It'll be okay."

Counting in a Dream, 2

That time I counted out of a dream, it wasn't at all clear which numbers I was counting.

Did I start with one? Did two come right after? Was I counting at all or merely chanting?

And for how long was I counting? When did I decide to stop counting? *Did* I decide to stop counting?

Or did the enveloping air, the approaching walls, and the entire widening room

leave me no choice?

The Little Fuzzy Rudolph

When you put in the batteries
its nose lights up green
its legs go back and forth
and out comes the music.
I hate medleys
but today, poor creature
poor mother
I am played upon but good.
Those legs are like a baby's
crawling inch by inch
unit-fractions
plodding along
the way we all do.
And his little pointy chin nods yes
every time I ask him "Are you cute?"
Yes, I am taken
in that way.
And I have to remind myself that he's not conscious
have to keep from taking him up and
not quite squeezing him
not quite breast-feeding him
only lifting him up off the floor
only telling him he doesn't have to light up
doesn't have to crawl
doesn't have to try try again.
"It's naptime," I can tell him
and whisk him away
wrap him in a blanket
take out the batteries
give his fuzzy little brain
a rest for awhile.

Arin-at-9 Grapples with Vegetarianism

Wants to know whether there's any way we can get the
 steak without killing the cow.
"Well," I suggest, "meat is muscles. We could take out just
 the muscles."
"But then the cow wouldn't be able to move."
"Well, we could use just one leg."
"Nah, the cow wouldn't like that. I know,"
he suddenly brightens up. "We could make doubling
machines. And then we could just use the cow's double."
"Sure." we continue. "Doubles of cows look like cows,
 sound like cows, and (above all) taste like cows."
And we could just keep killing and eating the doubles
 till they begin to think like cows.

Phone Number in a Dream: 2001

I retained each digit, each of the ten, but I never called, didn't have the nerve.

He was my dream-guy, he gave me his number, would have been happy to hear from me. But outside the dream he'd think me nuts.

It had a 9, a 2, and at least one 0, all ten are in my diary. I don't need it now but you, single friend, any single friend, you might want to try it, it might be the number of your dream-guy.

Or maybe you've dreamt that number too.

My First Dream of Him

At the quiet piano
over my trembling shoulder
he takes his sweet soft 'a.'
It's 'a' minor
and lower-case.
I begin to look up.
He begins to bend down.
Then he kisses, still soft, the top of my head.
I reach to keep that kiss.
He is still taking the 'a.'
The dream seems so real.
It says, "Yes it's time."
But soon I spin around
to look into his face.
And here the 'a' turns upper-case.
Too big. Too major.
And the dream becomes awash.
It says to me, "No
it is not yet time
for this."

Singing in a Dream

Well, it's more like humming.
Even more like groaning.
Some wood is warping, some rope straining.
Some boat is trying to escape the shore.

And I'm certainly not first soprano.
One low-C glissandos into some other low-C.
I'm a kid pretending to ice-skate
with neither skates nor ice.

All she has is rubber-soled sneaks
and the equally rubber-y floor.

Orchestra

I do solo all the time and duets once a week, Becky's violin to my piano, and I've played in trios but only once have I played in an orchestra. I'd just started Arts High and I guess they needed a pianist so arranged for me to try it out, or it to try me out.

Well, first, their orchestra was more like a band, a marching band, and second, the tall piano was facing a wall, I couldn't see the racket I was supposed to keep up with, it was shooting me again and again in the back.

I still remember the room. The wall that suffocating upright was along also contained the door, the door was to the left, and it was a regular classroom, not the auditorium. What I remember most: that was the last time.

Arts High loved me, loved my math, my writing, even my piano, but I guess they decided no, orchestra wasn't for me, nor I for it. And to this day orchestra is to me as trumpets were to little Mozart, too loud, too big, too much cheering, too much like sports, too many players, too many variables, not enough constants, not enough zeroes.

2004

This is the summer of dress-up.
Tops and bottoms of closets
five bags of bows and lace
things to cut and paste
into things I can't wait to try on.
This is the season of morn-to-night playing.
Don't bother me, it's the summer of my wedding
and I'm not grown up any more.

In Praise of Bathrooms

All through the kitchen lie unwashed dishes, pink brace-
 lets, and yesterday's *Times*.
All through the living room squat drums, bookbags, and
 someone else's jackets.
And through the entire house crawls the floor
kitty sheddings, occasional regurgitatings, and ordinary
 dust.
All through the house march walls that need repainting
 and appliances that need fixing.
But bathrooms are exactly the way they should be.
White decor, maybe white with exceptions
exceptions that I and no one else chose.
And bathroom floors are small, quick to clean, to inspect
 every square inch.
Bathroom walls also small, easily painted or cleaned.
Also, bathroom clutter just gets tossed into the wash.
True, bathroom sinks can crack, tiles can yellow, and
 plumbing can require plumbing.
But mostly, bathrooms are perfect little clubhouses,
 miniature hotel rooms.
We can sneak into them when we need perfection
when we need the world to be small.

Reading in a Dream, 2

The letters are upper-case.
And they're stick-figures.
They're also italics
though their slant is not constant.

They're not in a book.
They're on some low board.
Somebody posted them.
They're a vital sign
that everyone, not only my special brain
must obey.

Spellcheck

When I hand-write I expect a thin red line to appear under my pen, what appears will be other than what I choose to write, double consonants when I mean single, caps when I mean lower-case. Maybe I'll soon start expecting talkcheck, hello when I mean goodbye, silence when I mean tantrum.

And deedcheck. What I do will be instantly replaced by other doings. Maybe red doings. Not bloody, only red.

Quirky

I'm always mixing up solstice and equinox. I look it up
 and then forget again.
There seem to be certain things my brain refuses to know.

Hearing the radio, I don't always recognize a musical
 instrument. Is it violin, piano, flute? There are some parts
 of sounds my ears refuse to hear.

And I can't snap my fingers. Well, they snap but don't
 make noise.
There are some noises my body refuses to make.

Here

"Why are you here?" asks the smiling
intake guy for the routine colonoscopy.
The following is what I might answer:

Yeah, why am I here?
Now, you. You're always here.
Here is your work, your life.
Whereas here is anything but my work and life.
Here is very much not math, very much not thrifting,
 very much not Jon.
Only today am I here, for this, only this.
Why indeed am I here?
Why don't I just go home?

In Praise of Bathroom Chandeliers

The stars are too many to fit in this room.
But these tiny nightlights aren't.
They give no more light than the distant stars.
But bathrooms don't need much light.
And not only is it romantic, it's practical.
Now the top of the toilet simply shines.
Now there are no little spots on the sink.
And best of all, the floor.
We no longer have to wipe the floor.
With such good things happening by the ceiling
we don't have to worry about the floor.

Clarinet and Piano

Andrea got us the recording and it was a lot faster than
 we play it.
The notes were a-wash, the notes were a-whirr.
No more Sehnsucht, no more Angst.
Phrases became molecules, measures became atoms.
A whole new order of tiny, a whole new order of fast.
Now when we play it she'll go "pum pum pum"
take it up to tem-po.
She'll snap her fingers, tap her feet.
Even those arrivals–you know Brahms' arrivals
and those reachings, the ones I practice for hours
sometimes because I need to, sometimes because I want
 to
well, now you heard them now you don't
or maybe you never did.
I learned long ago
that poor people aren't necessarily pure
foreign children are just as American as American
 children
silence isn't golden nor stillness silver.
But I'd thought slow was slow.
I'd thought Brahms was Brahms.

Creating a Face in a Dream

They say you can't create a
face in a dream; whatever face
you dream is something from
your past. There's also a hoax
about This Man, whose face
appears in everyone's dreams.

Those features last night, and the tiger-lily hair, I swear I've
never seen them. Well, maybe the too-slight nose and chin,
they might be part of This Man's face. But the rest of that
face, I made it myself, my special brain created that face.

Sure as it fashions poems, sure as it fashions fashion, my
special brain fashioned that face, that special if rather creepy
face. In fact it fashioned two of them, one to my left, one
to my right. It sat between them, shaping and coloring that
whole silly show

from that dubious director's chair in the middle.

Two Pains

(1) Pain in a Dream

Pain in a dream is more like tickling.
A buzzing, a funny bone, maybe a spine.
Pain in a dream is like novocain.
We feel pressure, digging, and something very slow.
And we know darn well it's there.

(2) The Paradox of Pain in Reality

Pain is the immovable object against the irresistible force.
Or it's the immovable object being crushed.
Emotional tragedy is easy. We can simply ignore it.
But physical pain must be felt.
It can't and yet it is and has been.
When we're in pain the universe can't exist.
So what are we doing here?
Why can't we leave?

Doing in a Dream

You can dream you talk and walk and think.
And my special brain can dream it's having a baby.
It can even dream it's moving.
In real-life it's paralyzed but in dreams it's moving fast.
It can, yes, dream it's flying
dream it's floating, dream it's falling.
And it can, yes, dream it's reading.
It can dream it's doing all the things
it can't do in a dream.

Not a Poem, Merely Questions

How do I know I have a head?
 Just because everyone else near and far has a head. How
 do I know all the mirrors and photographs haven't been
 lying?
Every mirror, soon as I look into it, shows a head.
And every photograph has a head in it.
Who is it that arranges all this, that can keep abreast of so
 many mirrors and
photographs? Who is it that plants the same
 head in all those times and places?

And who is it that fixes it so, whenever my hands touch what
 I think is my head, whenever I run my forefinger along what
 I've been told is my nose
 fixes it so the feeling in my finger is consistent with what I
 see in mirrors and photographs?
When I was three months old, did I slowly
 wiggle my fingers and stare at them?
Is that when that one began its arranging?
And with what eyes did I stare?

The Body's Way

When doctors say "That's the body's way," they look tender, as though the body were a child. Doctors are in love with the body, any body, the way I'm in love with math, the way one can be in love with absolute truth.

If humankind were to evolve into not having bodies, doctors wouldn't like it. What?! no crust on tonsils, no infinitesimal tickles on scalps, nothing to puzzle, nothing to study, no polarities, no paradoxes

no bargaining, no mysterious ways.

Reading in a Dream, 3

Jon's brain is special.
It can read in a dream.
Well, that dream.

Well, just the answer sheet.
It can't read what anything
is the answer to.

Also, every answer
is exactly the same.

Still, my guy
was reading in a dream.
My special guy's
special brain
was reading in a dream.

Author Biography

Marion Deutsche Cohen is the author of 26 collections of poetry or memoir; her latest poetry collection is *New Heights in Non-Structure* (dancing girl press) about home-schooling and other ideas about engaging with children. She is also the author of two controversial memoirs about spousal chronic illness *Dirty Details: The Days and Nights of a Well Spouse* (Temple University Press), and *Still the End: Memoir of a Nursing Home Wife* (Unlimited Publishing), a trilogy diary of late-pregnancy loss, and of *Crossing the Equal Sign* (Plain View Press) about the experience of mathematics.

She teaches math and writing at Arcadia University in Glenside, PA, where she has developed the course, Mathematics in Literature. A poetry chapbook, *Truth and Beauty* about the interaction in that course among students and teacher, was released in 2016, from WordTech Editions. She is about to begin teaching the course at Drexel University. Other interests are classical piano, singing, Scrabble, thrift-shopping, four grown children, and five grands. Her website is marioncohen.net.

www.ingramcontent.com/pod-product-compliance
Lightning Source LLC
Chambersburg PA
CBHW051006060726
47593CB00017B/1093